BY JAMES S. KELLEY

THE NORTHWEST DIVISION

THE DENVER NUGGETS

THE UTAH JAZZ

THE MINNESOTA TIMBERWOLVES

THE PORTLAND TRAIL BLAZERS

THE SEATTLE SUPERSONICS

Published in the United States of America by
The Child's World® • 1980 Lookout Drive
Mankato, MN 56003-1705
800-599-READ • www.childsworld.com

ACKNOWLEDGEMENTS

The Child's World®: Mary Berendes,
Publishing Director

The Design Lab: Kathleen Petelinsek,
Design and Page Production

Manuscript consulting and photo research by
Shoreline Publishing Group LLC.

PHOTOS

Cover: Corbis
Interior photos: AP/Wide World: 10, 18, 22, 26;
Corbis: 4, 28; Reuters: 7, 8, 13, 14, 16, 21, 24,
30, 32

**LIBRARY OF CONGRESS
CATALOGING-IN-PUBLICATION DATA**

Kelley, James S., 1960–

The Northwest division / by James S. Kelley.

   p. cm. – (Above the rim)

Includes bibliographical references and index.

ISBN 978-1-59296-983-8 (library bound : alk.
paper)

1. National Basketball Association–History–
Juvenile literature.

2. Basketball–West (U.S.)–History–Juvenile
literature. I. Title. II. Series.

GV885.515.N37K445 2008

796.323'640973–dc22   2007034763

CONTENTS

*On the cover: Denver Nuggets forward
Carmelo Anthony was the NBA's second-
leading scorer in 2006–07, when he
averaged 28.9 points per game.*

INTRODUCTION

The Northwest Division of the National Basketball Association features some of the brightest young stars in basketball.

Utah's Carlos Boozer was only 25 years old when he led the Jazz to the division title during the 2006–07 season. Twenty-two-year-old Carmelo Anthony and the Denver Nuggets were close behind. And 19-year-old rookies Greg Oden (Portland) and Kevin Durant (Seattle) hope to restore their new teams to prior heights.

The "old man" on the block is 27-year-old Ricky Davis in Minnesota. The Timberwolves hope that he can help make up for the loss of All-Star forward Kevin Garnett, who was traded to Boston after the 2006–07 season.

Will any of these stars align to bring a Northwest Division **franchise** an NBA championship? Read on, and you can decide for yourself!

CHAPTER ONE

THE DENVER NUGGETS

High-flying David Thompson was an All-Star while playing for the Nuggets.

In Carmelo Anthony and Allen Iverson, Denver's roster actually features two superstars. The franchise hopes that the pair can help the Nuggets strike gold: a league championship. In its 40 years of play entering 2007–08, Denver has not won a title. But the Nuggets have featured some very good teams and very good players in a history that began in the old American Basketball Association (ABA) in 1967.

You may have seen pictures of ABA games. The league was famous for using a red, white, and blue basketball during its nine seasons from 1967–68 to 1975–76. Denver was one of the best teams in the history of the ABA. The franchise won three division championships and advanced to the **playoffs** seven times. In 1976, the ABA disbanded. Four of its franchises, though—the Nuggets, the Indiana Pacers, the New York Nets, and the San Antonio Spurs—joined the NBA.

With stars such as center Dan Issel, forward Bobby Jones, and guard David Thompson, Denver remained successful in its new league. The Nuggets even won a division championship (they played in the Midwest Division at the time) their very first season in the NBA. Thompson, who was called "Skywalker" for his gravity-defying dunks, was a prolific scorer. He averaged more than 25 points per game four times in his seven seasons in Denver.

The Nuggets were a high-scoring team in their early years. One season (1981–82), they set an NBA record by averaging 126.5 points per game. Unfortunately, they set another record for

Denver's ABA team was originally known as the Rockets. But when it looked like the Rockets were going to join the NBA, they had to change their name. That's because the NBA already had the Houston Rockets.

points allowed, 126.0 per game, and lost in the first round of the playoffs.

That started a trend. In 1982–83, forwards Alex English (28.4 points per game) and Kiki Vandeweghe (26.7) finished one-two in the NBA in scoring, but the Nuggets, who went 45–37 during the regular season, were eliminated in the second round of the playoffs. In fact, Denver made the playoffs nine consecutive seasons under coach Doug Moe beginning in 1981–82. The Nuggets made it past the conference semifinals only once, though. That came in 1984–85, when the team won 52 regular-season games and captured the division title. Denver then beat San Antonio and Utah in the playoffs before being stopped by the eventual-NBA-champion Lakers in five games in the conference finals.

After that, postseason appearances suddenly were harder to come by. Beginning in 1990–91, Denver finished above the **.500 mark** only one time in a 13-season span. One highlight of the 1990s, though, was the play of Dikembe Mutombo, a 7-foot-2 center from the Democratic Republic of the Congo. He led the league in blocked shots for three consecutive seasons, was twice named to the All-Star team, and was named the league's Defensive Player of the Year for the 1994–95 season.

The Nuggets made the playoffs as the eighth-rated (and lowest-rated) team in 1993–94. They stunned Seattle three games to two to become the first No. 8 team to beat a No. 1 in the postseason.

In December of 1983, the Nuggets and the Pistons played the highest-scoring game in NBA history. Detroit won 186–184 in three overtimes.

In 2003, the Nuggets chose Anthony with the third pick of the **draft**, and they immediately got better. Anthony averaged a team-leading 21.0 points per game and was a league All-Rookie first-team selection. Denver improved from 17 wins in 2002–03 to 43 wins in 2003–04, and made the playoffs.

With Anthony in the lineup, the Nuggets made the postseason each of the next two years, too. But they could not get out of the first round. So in December of 2006, the club traded for Iverson. He is a prolific scorer and a former NBA MVP who led the Philadephia 76ers to the **NBA Finals** in 2000–01.

The Nuggets finished with 45 wins during the 2006–07 regular season. They still lost in the opening round of the 2007 playoffs, though. But with Anthony and Iverson paired together for a full season beginning in 2007–08, the franchise hopes that one day soon it will finally be able to hang a championship banner in Denver.

Carmelo Anthony (left) and Allen Iverson give the Nuggets a powerful one-two punch.

CHAPTER TWO

THE MINNESOTA TIMBERWOLVES

One of the highlights of the T-Wolves' history was their hard-fought playoff win over the Nuggets in 2004.

Few NBA teams have been as identifiable with one player as the Minnesota Timberwolves have been with forward Kevin Garnett. He was the face of the franchise for more than a decade after he first joined the club directly out of high school in 1995. So that made it a big shock when the Timberwolves decided to part ways with Garnett before the 2007–08 season. They traded him to the Boston Celtics in a huge deal that brought five players and two future draft picks to the Timberwolves. It maked the beginning of a brand-new era in Minnesota.

Before Garnett's arrival, the T-Wolves, as the club is often called, were a typical **expansion team**. Minnesota, which began play in the 1989–1990 season, averaged only 21 wins per season in its first six years. Still, the club enjoyed wild support from its fans. In fact, when the T-Wolves made their NBA debut at home, a crowd of 35,427 poured into the Metrodome. (The spacious home of football's Minnesota Vikings and baseball's Minnesota Twins was their temporary home before moving into the Target Center in 1990–91.) For the year, Minnesota's average attendance of 26,160 fans per game set an NBA record.

The fans stayed true to the T-Wolves despite their struggles, and despite the lack of a star attraction in the early years. But their loyalty was rewarded in 1995. That year, Garnett, a senior at Farragut Academy in Chicago, made himself eligible for the NBA draft. Many teams were skeptical; 20 years had passed since a high school player had jumped directly to the NBA. Kevin McHale, the former Boston

There are approximately 1,275 timberwolves in the continental United States; about 1,200 of them live in Minnesota.

Celtics' Hall-of-Fame forward who was then (and still is) the T-Wolves' general manager, took a chance on Garnett. He selected the 18-year-old with the fifth overall pick in the draft.

McHale's gamble paid off. Garnett was the **prototype** of the modern player. He was nearly 7 feet tall, but could dribble like a point guard, shoot like an off-guard, and rebound and defend like a power forward. In 1996–97, he made the **Western Conference** All-Star squad for the first of 10 times through 2007.

More importantly, the T-Wolves also made the playoffs for the first time in 1996–97. Coached by Flip Saunders, who was in his first full season with the team, and led by Garnett, forward Tom Gugliotta, and point guard Stephon Marbury, Minnesota went 40–42. That wasn't great, but it was good enough for third place in the Midwest Division.

In the playoffs, the Rockets made quick work of the T-Wolves, sweeping them in the first round of the playoffs. That began a **bittersweet** string for Minnesota. The T-Wolves made the playoffs each of the next seven seasons, too, but went out in the first round six more times. Finally, they won a postseason series for the first time in 2003–04. That year, Minnesota beat Denver in the opening round and then Sacramento in the next round of the

Kevin Garnett set a T-Wolves' record when he scored 47 points in a game against the Phoenix Suns in January of 2005.

playoffs before falling to the Lakers in six games in the conference finals.

Garnett was still the star. In fact, he was named the NBA's MVP that season after averaging 24.2 points per game. But most of his teammates were new. In 1998, Garnett had been signed to the largest con-

In April of 1990, the
T-Wolves hosted
the Denver Nuggets
before 49,551 fans
at the Metrodome.
It was the third-
largest crowd to
see an NBA game.

tract in NBA history, worth approximately $120 million. Jealousy ensued.

Marbury, lightning-quick and a great **assists** creator, was unhappy about playing second fiddle to Garnett. He was traded. Gugliotta, a **free agent**, signed with the Phoenix Suns in '98 for far more cash than Minnesota was willing—or able—to pay him.

In 1999, the T-Wolves drafted a legitimate second scoring option. Wally Szczerbiak [ZER-bee-ack], a 6-foot-7 forward, was named to the All-Rookie first team. Later, veteran guards Sam Cassell and Latrell Sprewell played key roles on the 2003–04 team that delivered the T-Wolves' first division championship.

That excellent season raised expectations—and the T-Wolves have been unable to meet them. They tumbled out of the playoffs each of the next three years and had a revolving door of coaches. Then the unthinkable happened after a 32–50 season in 2006–07: Garnett was traded.

Garnett's departure left guard and forward Ricky Davis as the team's top returning scorer. He averaged 17.0 points per game in 2006–07. Minnesota also was counting on some of the players the club acquired from Boston to be big contributors.

For the first time since their franchise face arrived more than a decade earlier, the T-Wolves faced an uncertain future.

CHAPTER THREE

THE PORTLAND TRAIL BLAZERS

Greg Oden won't play until 2008–09, but the club hopes he'll prove to be a good fit for them.

The Portland Trail Blazers didn't have very many victories in 2006–07. They won only 32 of 82 regular-season games and finished tied for third place in the Northwest Division, 19 games behind first-place Utah. But the Blazers got one very important win after the season. That's when they won the NBA Draft Lottery and were awarded the first overall pick in the June 2007 selection process. With the choice, Portland took acclaimed center Greg Oden of Ohio State. Oden had knee surgery and was expected to miss the entire 2007–08 NBA season, but the Trail Blazers hope that he eventually will do what another big man—center Bill Walton—did for the franchise more than 30 years earlier.

The Trail Blazers got their nickname from the 1800s explorations of the famous Lewis and Clark. Their western travels took them into what is now the northwest tip of Oregon.

In the summer of 1974, Portland was a young, struggling franchise. The Trail Blazers had managed just a 27–55 record in their fourth season in the league. But with the first pick of the draft, they chose the 6-foot-11 Walton, who had led the UCLA Bruins to a pair of college championships.

Walton was injured much of his first two seasons, but the Trail Blazers clearly were better when he was in the lineup. Then, in 1976–77, he played in most of the team's games. He averaged 21.4 points and 16.5 rebounds per game. He had a lot of help, too, from players such as forward Maurice Lucas and guards Dave Twardzik and Lionel Hollins. The Trail Blazers, under first-year coach Jack Ramsey, posted their first winning record (49–33) and made the playoffs.

Hall-of-Famer Clyde Drexler wouldn't let anything—or anyone—come between him and the basket.

For nearly 20 years from the championship season of 1977 until the mid-1990s, the Trail Blazers sold out every home game.

In the postseason, Portland took the league by surprise. After beating the Bulls and Nuggets, the Trail Blazers swept the Lakers in four games in the conference championship. They followed that up with a six-game victory over the 76ers in the NBA Finals. In just their seventh season, the Trail Blazers were NBA champions.

Walton had more injury problems and played just one more season in Portland before making stops in three other cities in his Hall of Fame career. And though the Trail Blazers have not won a title since, their championship season began a long run of excellence. Portland made the playoffs all but one time in the 27 seasons from 1976–77 to 2002–03.

Along the way, the club has featured some tremendous players. In 1983, the team drafted Clyde "the Glide" Drexler, who would become a perennial All-Star. He played 11 1/2 years in Portland and would be a key part of the Blazers' return to the NBA Finals in 1989–90. (The Pistons won the series in five games.)

In 1995, the club moved from the Portland Memorial Coliseum to its jazzy new digs, the Rose Garden. The same season, Arvydas Sabonis, a 31-year-old Lithuanian rookie center who had played six years in the Spanish League, came to play in Portland.

Damon Stoudamire, a Portland native, became the Blazers' point guard in 1997–98. The following year, Portland made it to the Western Conference Finals. In 1999–2000, the Blazers picked up veteran small forward Scottie Pippen and made it to the Western Conference Finals before losing to the Lakers in Game 7.

Since then, the team has not won a postseason series. In fact, the club has not made it to the playoffs or posted a winning record since 2002–03. But that's where the rookie Oden comes in. He was a superstar in his lone season of college at Ohio State, where he led the Buckeyes to the championship game of the NCAA tournament.

Oden joins several outstanding young players—such as forward Zach Randolph and guard Brandon Roy—already on the Trail Blazers' roster. Together, they give the club a promising future.

Clyde Drexler's uniform number (22) has been retired not only by the Trail Blazers, but also by the NBA's Houston Rockets and college basketball's Houston Cougars.

Brandon Roy averaged 16.8 points per game en route to NBA Rookie of the Year honors in 2006–07.

CHAPTER FOUR

THE SEATTLE SUPERSONICS

Head coach Lenny Wilkens (left) and captain Fred Brown were all smiles after Seattle won the 1979 title.

With a new head coach, a rookie superstar in the making, and a revamped roster, the SuperSonics began a new chapter in their history in 2007–08. They hope they will match some of the success

The SuperSonics got their nickname from Seattle's top industry in the late 1960s: jet aircraft manufacturing. A local schoolteacher and his son were the first to suggest the name in a public contest.

of past Seattle teams. The Sonics (as the club often is called) can boast of 22 play-off seasons, five division championships, and one NBA title in a history that began in 1967–68.

Seattle was an expansion team that season in the NBA's Western Division. Most expansion teams have a hard time at first, and the Sonics were no exception. Toward the end of the 1970–71 season, however, the club got its first **bona fide** superstar when high-scoring forward Spencer Haywood joined the club. Haywood and guard Lenny Wilkens, who also was the coach, helped the team post a winning record for the first time in 1971–72.

Wilkens left after that season in a trade, but he returned as a coach only in 1977–78. By then, the Sonics had built their first high-quality team, which included long-range scoring threat Fred Brown, guard Slick Watts, and rookie center Jack Sikma. The Sonics made it to the NBA Finals, where they forced the Washington Bullets to Game 7 before losing.

In 1978–79, the Sonics won the NBA title after winning more than 50 games (52) and winning their first division title (the Pacific Division, which was formed in 1970). In the NBA Finals, they lost the first game to Washington and then won the next four games. Wilkens

Gary Payton's leadership and ball-handling skills made him a fan favorite in Seattle.

The Sonics and the Los Angeles Clippers opened the regular season in 2003–04 by playing two games in Japan. Seattle won them both.

stayed on as coach through 1984–85 before moving to the front office.

Over the next several years, Seattle featured some good players such as forwards Tom Chambers and Xavier McDaniel, three-point shooter Dale Ellis, and point guard Nate McMillan. But the team had only moderate success until point guard Gary Payton and head coach George Karl arrived in the early 1990s.

Karl's pressing, trapping, double-teaming outfit added veteran forward Sam Perkins, forward Detlef Schrempf, and guard Hersey Hawkins. In 1993–94, Seattle won an NBA-best 63 games during the regular season, but was upset in the first round of the playoffs. Two years later, the Sonics won 64 regular-season games en route to the NBA Finals, where they lost to Michael Jordan and the Chicago Bulls in six games. In 1997–98, Karl's final year, the Sonics went 61–21. They became the third NBA team ever to win 55 games or more in six consecutive seasons.

It also marked the sixth consecutive year that Seattle finished in first or second place in the division. (The Sonics and Lakers tied for first in the Pacific Division that year.) But the next six years all resulted in fourth- or fifth-place finishes.

Finally, the team broke the string with a surprising season in 2004–05. With all-stars Ray Allen and Rashard Lewis leading

the way, and former point guard McMillan as coach, Seattle won 52 games during the regular season. They won the first Northwest Division title and advanced to the second round of the playoffs.

Kevin Durant went right to work in the NBA Summer League after the Sonics drafted him in 2007.

"Downtown" Fred Brown holds the club record of 58 points in a game against the Warriors in 1974.

The Sonics could not build on that success, however, over the next two seasons. Their 31–51 mark in 2006–07 was one of the worst in their history. So management decided to go in another direction.

For 2007–08, the Sonics brought in P.J. Carlesimo as coach. (P.J. had coached previously in Portland and Golden State.) The team traded Allen and Lewis. And the club selected forward Kevin Durant with the second overall pick of the draft.

The high-flying Durant was a big-time player in his lone season in college at Texas. Although he was just an 18-year-old freshman at the start of 2006–07, Kevin was one of only three college players to average more than 20 points (he averaged 25.8) and 10 rebounds (11.1) that season. He was the college player of the year. He carried the Longhorns to the second round of the NCAA basketball tournament before deciding to turn pro.

Another highly touted rookie is forward Jeff Green. The Celtics chose the former Georgetown star with the fifth overall pick of the 2007 draft. They they traded him to Seattle in the deal that sent Allen to Boston.

The Sonics hope that Durant and Green form the cornerstone of an excellent team for many years to come.

CHAPTER FIVE

THE UTAH JAZZ

Pete Maravich was the Jazz' biggest star during the franchise's time in New Orleans.

The origins of the Jazz franchise date back to the 1970s. But after the departure of two of the greatest players in NBA history in the early 2000s—forward Karl Malone and guard John Stockton—the club found itself starting all over again. That made the team's Northwest Division championship in 2006–07 especially sweet.

The Jazz came into the league as an expansion franchise in New Orleans in 1974. Pete Maravich, who played college basketball at nearby Louisiana State University, was the team's first star. Pete led the league in scoring in 1976–77 by averaging 31.1 points per game. On one evening that season, Maravich scored 68 points against the New York Knicks.

The Jazz got their nickname from the signature music of New Orleans, the city in which the franchise originated in 1974. When the team moved to Utah in 1979, it kept the name.

The club had little success in New Orleans, however. It didn't win many games and didn't build much of a following. So in 1979, the franchise moved to Salt Lake City, Utah.

The 1983–84 season was one of many firsts for the Jazz. Led by colorful coach Frank Layden, Utah won the Midwest Division (45–37) for the first time. During that season, the Jazz became the first and only team to have four different players lead the league in a major statistical category. Adrian Dantley led the league in scoring (30.6 points per game), and Darrell Griffith had the highest percentage in the NBA in three-point field-goals (.361). Guard Rickey Green led the league in steals (2.65 per game). Big 7-foot-4 center Mark Eaton led the league in blocked shots (4.28 per game).

Guard John Stockton (left) and forward Karl Malone spelled double-trouble for Jazz opponents.

The Jazz have featured some legendary players with colorful nicknames, such Karl "The Mailman" Malone, "Pistol Pete" Maravich, and Darrell "Dr. Dunkenstein" Griffith.

Before the next season began, the Jazz drafted Stockton. Malone arrived one year after that. For the next 18 seasons, they were fixtures in Utah's lineup. No two NBA players ever were teammates for a longer stretch. Together, they helped make the Jazz a perennial championship contender.

Individually, Stockton and Malone rewrote the NBA record book. A 6-foot-1 point guard, Stockton is the league's all-time leader in assists (15,806) and steals (3,625). The 6-foot-9 Malone is number one all-time in free throws made (9,787) and attempted (13,188), is sixth in total rebounds (14,968), and 10th in scoring average (25.0 points per game). He is number two in total points (36,928 points).

Stockton and Malone led the Jazz to five Midwest Division titles (they tied for a sixth in 1989–90 with San Antonio) and two trips to the NBA Finals. Those journeys, in 1997 and 1998, were spoiled by the incredible Michael Jordan and the Chicago Bulls. But no team ever put more of a scare into the Bulls than the Jazz.

After the 2002–03 season, Stockton retired from basketball. Malone left as a free agent to join the rival Los Angeles Lakers. So the Jazz had to begin rebuilding their team. The job was left to head coach Jerry Sloan, who first had arrived during the 1988–89 season.

Initially, Utah struggled. In the first
year after the Stockton-Malone era, the
Jazz managed to win 42 games, although
they missed the playoffs. In 2004–05—the
first season of the Northwest Division—
Utah went just 26–56 and finished in last
place. Then came a 41–41 season.

Guard John Stockton and forward Karl Malone starred in front of the hometown fans at the Delta Center in the 1993 NBA All-Star Game. They shared MVP honors after leading the West team to a 135–132 victory.

Things were different from the very beginning in 2006–07, though. The Jazz got off to the best start in the NBA that season: 12 wins in their first 13 games. By season's end, they were atop the Northwest Division with a 51–31 record. In the playoffs, Utah beat Houston in an exciting seven-game series in the opening round. In the next round, the Jazz faced Golden State, which was riding high after an emotional upset of the Dallas Mavericks. But Utah won that series, too, needing only five games. Finally, the eventual-champion San Antonio Spurs proved to be too much for Utah in the conference finals, ending the Jazz' season in five games.

Still, the season was a success. Utah had become one of the NBA's best teams once again. Along the way, forward Carlos Boozer emerged as one of the league's top players. He averaged 20.9 points and 11.7 rebounds per game. Center Mehmet Okur, a native of Turkey, averaged 17.6 points and 7.2 rebounds per game.

Early in the 2006–07 season, Sloan became just the fourth NBA coach to win 1,000 games in his career. He completed his 19th year at the helm. No other current coach in the four major American sports—basketball, football, baseball, and hockey—had been with the same team for that long.

1970
The Portland Trail Blazers are founded

1976
The Denver Nuggets join the NBA

1979
The SuperSonics win their first Pacific Division title and the NBA title

1960

1970

1980

1983
Utah wins a division title and qualifies for the playoff for the first time

1967
Seattle joins the NBA as an expansion team, and Denver, then known as the Rockets, begins play in the American Basketball Association (ABA)

1977
Portland wins the NBA title in the franchise's seventh year, defeating Philadelphia 4–2 in the finals

1974
The Utah Jazz are founded

1989
The Minnesota Timberwolves join the NBA

2005
Seattle wins the division championship in the Northwest's first year

1990

2000

2010

2007
The Jazz win their first division title in seven years and advance to the Western Conference finals

2003
Minnesota wins a division title for the first time

TEAM RECORDS
(through 2006–07)

TEAM	ALL-TIME RECORD	NBA TITLES (MOST RECENT)	NUMBER OF TIMES IN PLAYOFFS	TOP COACH (WINS)
Denver	*1,575–1,679	0	*25	Doug Moe (432)
Minnesota	627–817	0	8	Flip Saunders (411)
Portland	1,588–1,414	1 (1976–77)	26	Jack Ramsey (453)
Seattle	1,725–1,523	1 (1978–79)	22	Lenny Wilkens (478)
Utah	1,439–1,235	0	21	Jerry Sloan (941)

*includes ABA

MEMBERS OF THE NAISMITH MEMORIAL NATIONAL BASKETBALL HALL OF FAME

DENVER

PLAYER	POSITION	DATE INDUCTED
Larry Brown	Coach	2002
Alex English	Forward	1997
Dan Issel	Center	1993
John McLendon	Coach	1979
David Thompson	Guard	1996

PORTLAND

PLAYER	POSITION	DATE INDUCTED
Clyde Drexler	Guard	2004
Drazen Petrovic	Guard	2002
Jack Ramsay	Coach	1992
Bill Walton	Center	1993
Lenny Wilkens	Guard/Coach	1989

MINNESOTA

Note: Minnesota does not have any members of the Hall of Fame (yet!).

NORTHWEST DIVISION CAREER LEADERS
(through 2006–07)

TEAM	CATEGORY	NAME (YEARS WITH TEAM)	TOTAL
Denver	Points	Alex English (1980–1990)	21,645
	Rebounds	Dan Issel (1975–1985)	6,630
Minnesota	Points	Kevin Garnett (1995–2007)	19,041
	Rebounds	Kevin Garnett (1995–2007)	10,542
Portland	Points	Clyde Drexler (1983–1995)	18,040
	Rebounds	Clyde Drexler (1983–1995)	5,339
Seattle	Points	Gary Payton (1990–2002)	18,207
	Rebounds	Jack Sikma (1977–1986)	7,729
Utah	Points	Karl Malone (1985–2003)	36,374
	Rebounds	Karl Malone (1985–2003)	14,601

SEATTLE

PLAYER	POSITION	DATE INDUCTED
David Thompson	Forward	1996
Lenny Wilkens	Guard/Coach	1989

UTAH

PLAYER	POSITION	DATE INDUCTED
Gail Goodrich	Guard	1996
Pete Maravich	Guard	1987

.500 mark—the same number of wins as losses; .500 is a winning percentage, which is calculated by dividing the number of victories by the total number of games

assists—passes that come immediately before a player makes a basket

bittersweet—something that makes a person both happy and sad

bona fide—genuine or authentic

draft—the annual selection of college players by a professional sports league

expansion team—a new franchise that starts from scratch

franchise—more than just the team, it is the entire organization that is a member of a professional sports league

free agent—an athlete who has finished his contract with one team and is eligible to sign with another

NBA Finals—a seven-game series between the winners of the NBA's Eastern and Western Conference championships

playoffs—a four-level postseason elimination tournament involving eight teams from each conference; levels include two rounds of divisional playoffs, a conference championship round, and the NBA Finals (all series are best-of-seven games)

prototype—an original on which later versions are patterned

Western Conference—one-half of the NBA, the Western Conference includes three divisions: the Northwest, Pacific, and Southwest. The Eastern Conference includes the other three divisions: Atlantic, Central, and Southeast.

Books

Frisch, Aaron. *The Story of the Portland Trail Blazers*. Mankato, Minn.: Creative Education, 2006.

Gilbert, Sara. *The Story of the Minnesota Timberwolves*. Mankato, Minn.: Creative Education, 2006.

Hareas, John. *Basketball*. New York: DK Publishers, 2005.

Hudson, David L. *Basketball's Most Wanted II: The Top 10 Book of More Hotshot Hoopsters, Double Dribbles, and Roundball Oddities*. Washington, D.C.: Potomac Books, Inc., 2005.

Leboutillier, Nate. *The Story of the Denver Nuggets*. Mankato, Minn.: Creative Education, 2006.

Leboutillier, Nate. *The Story of the Seattle SuperSonics*. Mankato, Minn.: Creative Education, 2006.

Leboutillier, Nate. *The Story of the Utah Jazz*. Mankato, Minn.: Creative Education, 2006.

Owens, Tom. *Basketball Arenas*. Brookfield, Conn.: Millbrook Press, 2002.

On the Web

Visit our Web page for lots of links about the Northwest Division teams: *http://www.childsworld.com/links*

Note to Parents, Teachers, and Librarians: We routinely verify our Web links to make sure they are safe, active sites—so encourage your readers to check them out!

ABOUT THE AUTHORS

James S. Kelley is the pseudonym for a group of veteran sportswriters who collaborated on this series. Among them, they have worked for *Sports Illustrated*, the National Football League, and NBC Sports. They have written more than a dozen other books for young readers on a wide variety of sports.